D1137857

How did I Begin?

by Mick Manning
and Brita Granström

W
FRANKLIN WATTS
LONDON • SYDNEY

Bristol Library Service
AN 3072619 0

How did I begin?

You began with a special cuddle
between your mum and dad.
But after this cuddle you didn't
just pop out into the world...
their cuddle was only the beginning.
It took nine months before you
were ready to be born.

How was I made?
As they cuddled, your dad's sperms swam inside your mum and met up with one of her eggs.
What are sperms and eggs?

Sperms are your dad's half of the recipe that makes a baby. They have a head and a tail and they swim like tiny tadpoles.

Eggs are your mum's half of the recipe. Mum's body produces one egg every month. Eggs are as tiny as this full stop.

As they cuddled, your dad's penis moved gently inside your mum's vagina and the sperms flowed out.

Your dad's sperms swam like crazy when they got inside your mum – they were searching for something – it was like a treasure hunt.

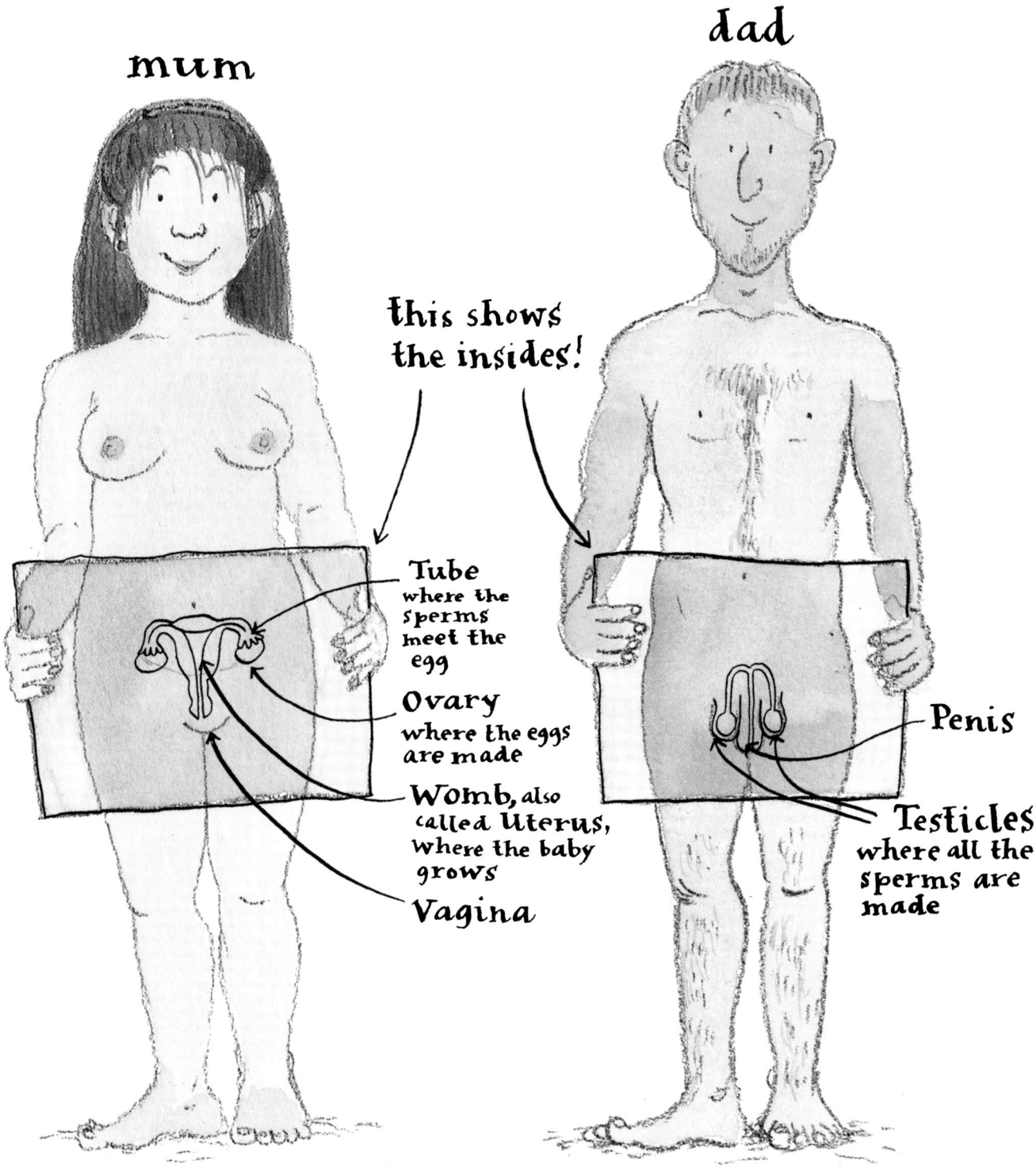

They found what they were looking for – they met mum's egg moving towards them down a long dark tunnel!
One sperm burrowed inside the egg and the egg made a tough skin to keep out the other sperms.

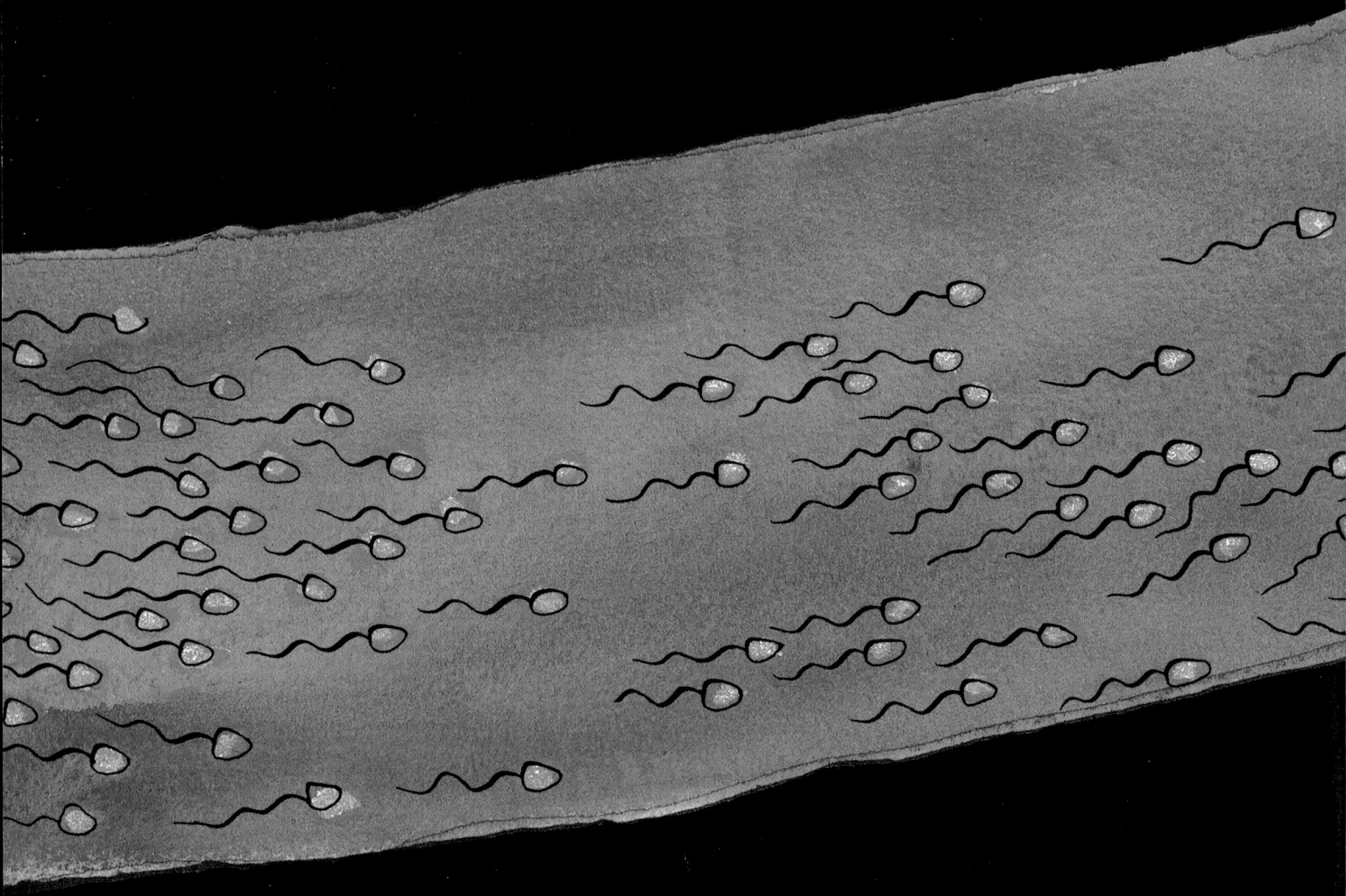

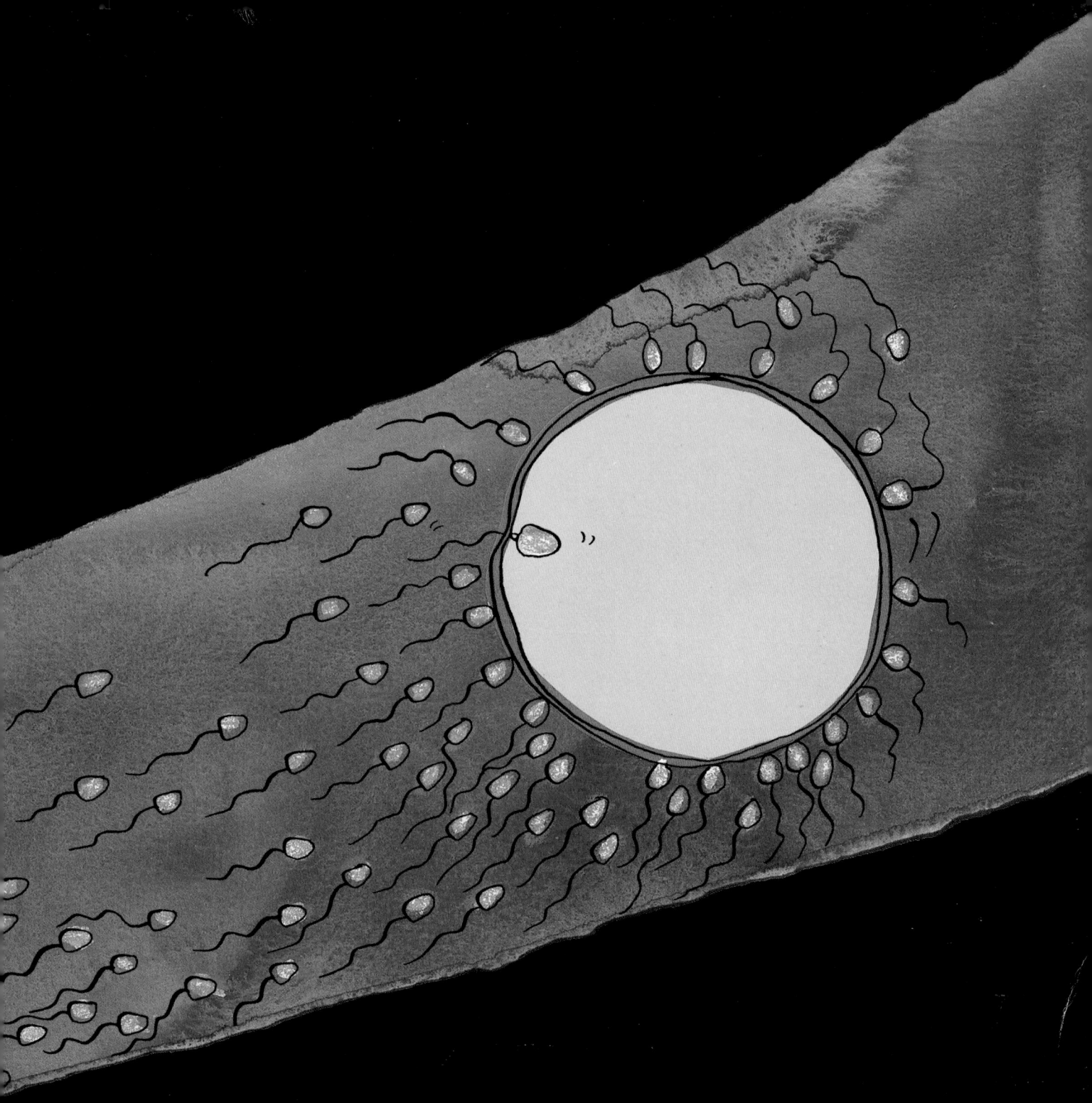

This is the split second you began!

Only one sperm out of millions
wins the race to make you.
That means you are a winner
from the second you are made!

Together the winning sperm and
your mum's egg made your first
living cell.

A cell is a sort of living building brick.

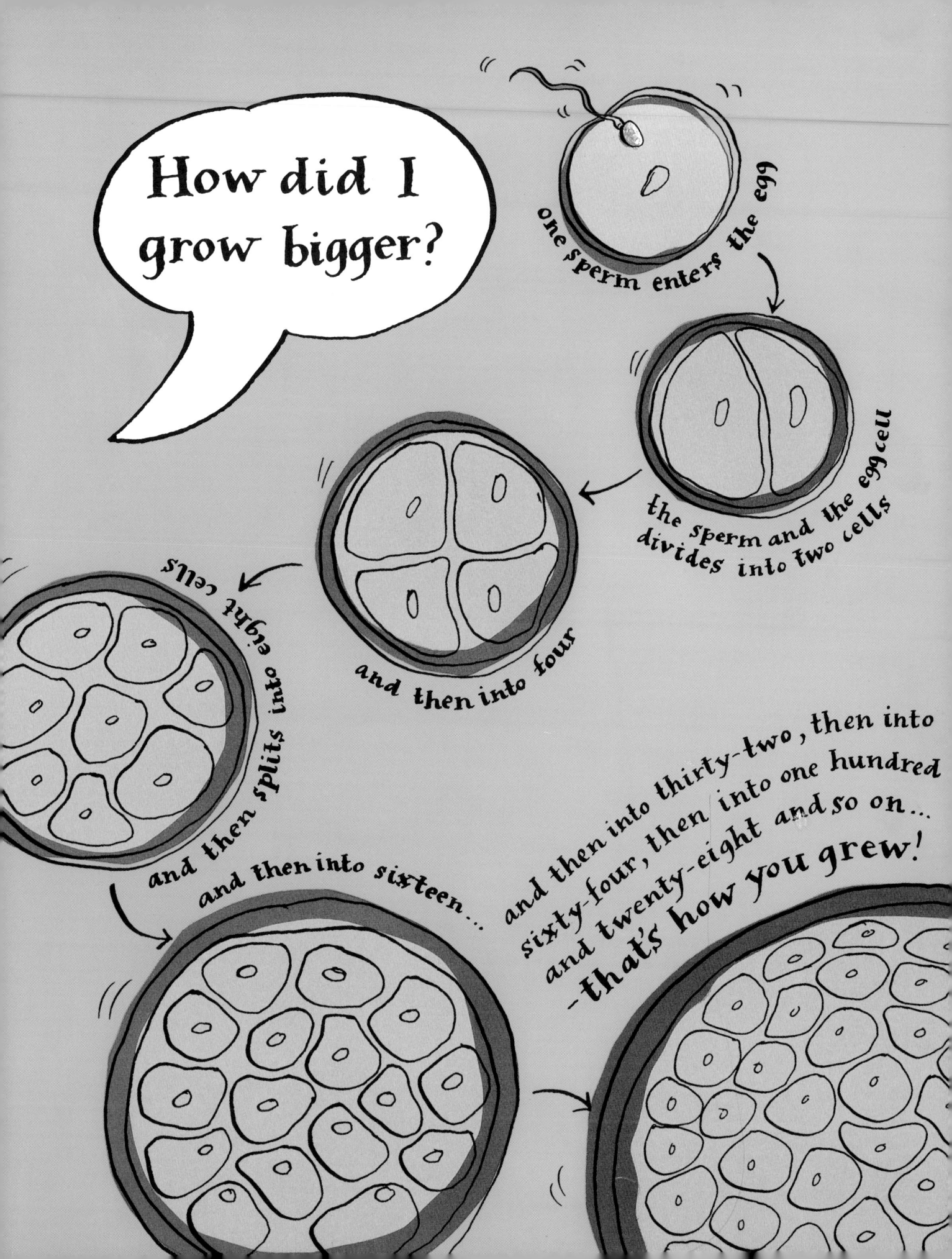
How did I grow bigger?
one sperm enters the egg
the sperm and the egg cell divides into two cells
and then into four
and then splits into eight cells
and then into sixteen...
and then into thirty-two, then into sixty-four, then into one hundred and twenty-eight and so on...
-that's how you grew!

What makes me look like I do?

Each cell contains chromosomes which are like building instructions to make you.

You get 23 chromosomes from your mum's egg and 23 from your dad's sperm.

That's why people say, "You have got your mum's eyes" or, "You have your dad's nose."

= dad

= mum

A baby's cells have 46 chromosomes, 23 from dad and 23 from mum.

How do twins happen?

If two sperms find two eggs then two babies grow up next to each other!

Sometimes the first cell divides and grows into two separate babies – they are called identical twins and they look almost the same.

As you began to grow, the tiny ball of cells that was you travelled into a warm, dark place called the womb and continued to grow.

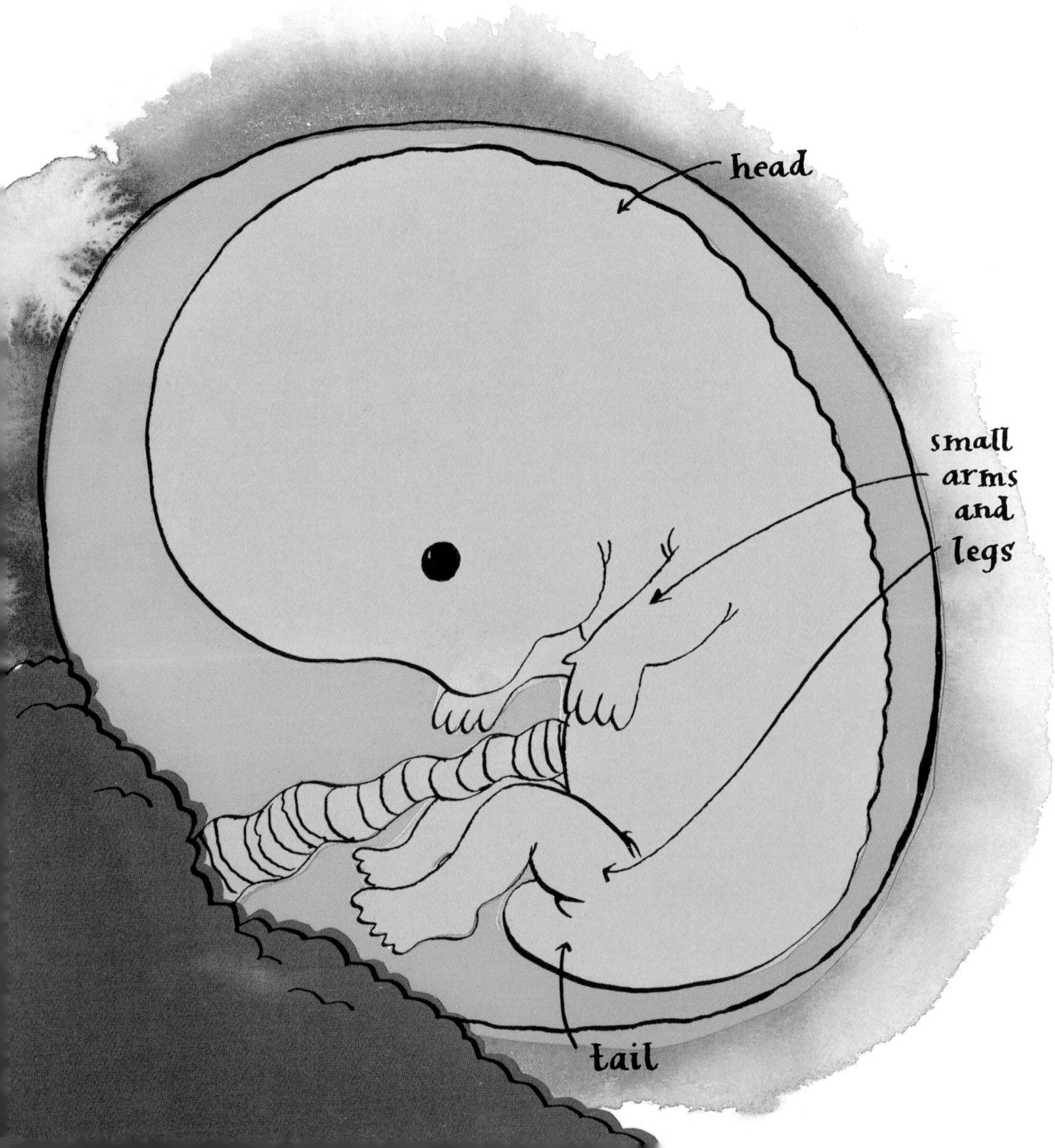

After a few weeks you had a head end and a tail end. After five weeks your tiny arms and legs began to grow.

Your mum may have visited a hospital to check you were OK. The doctors and nurses would make sure you were well.

Perhaps a machine called an ultrasound scanner took a photo of you inside your mum.

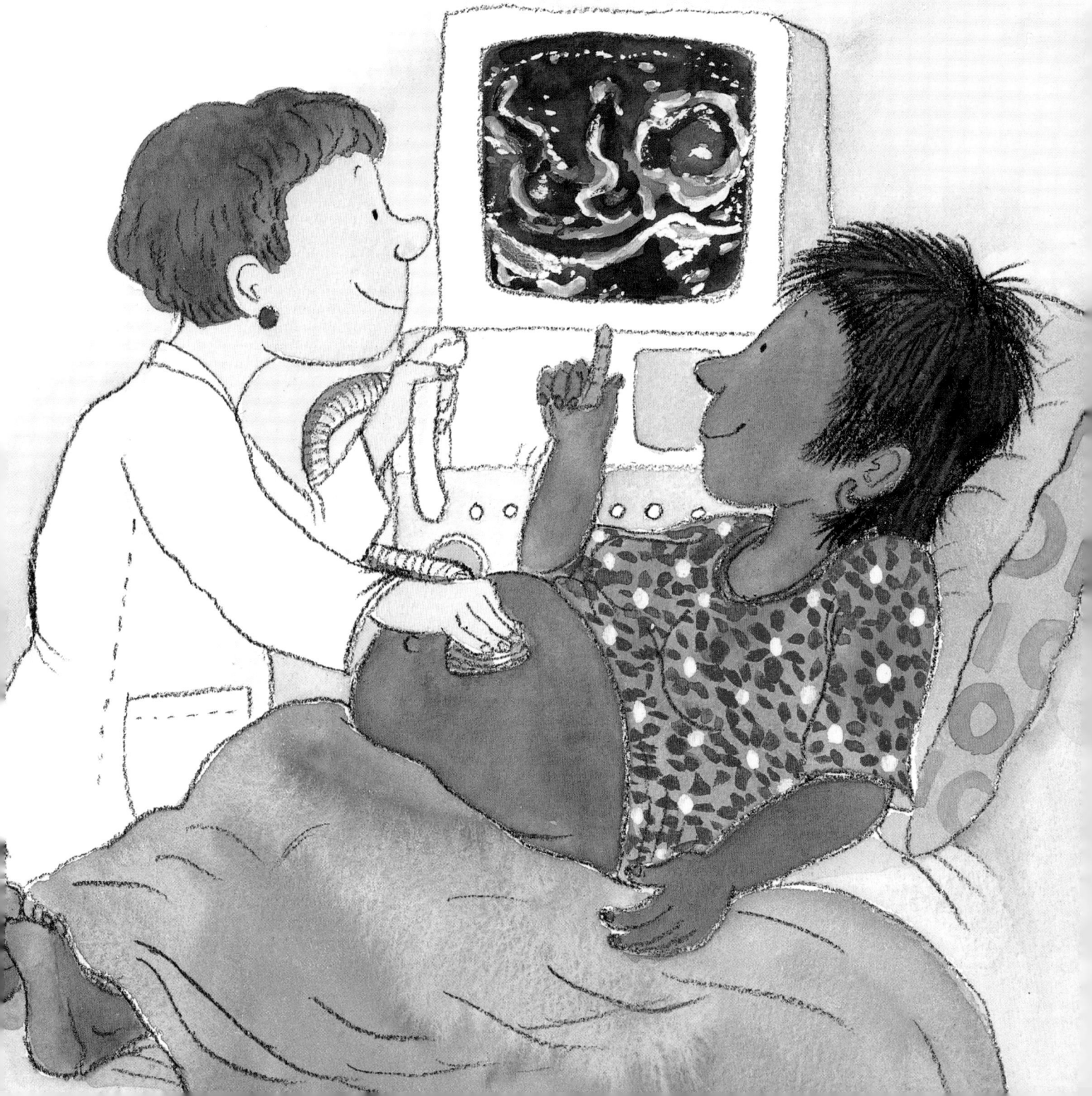

How did I breathe?

You didn't need to breathe inside your mum, all your nourishment and oxygen came in her bloodstream through a tube that joined you to her.

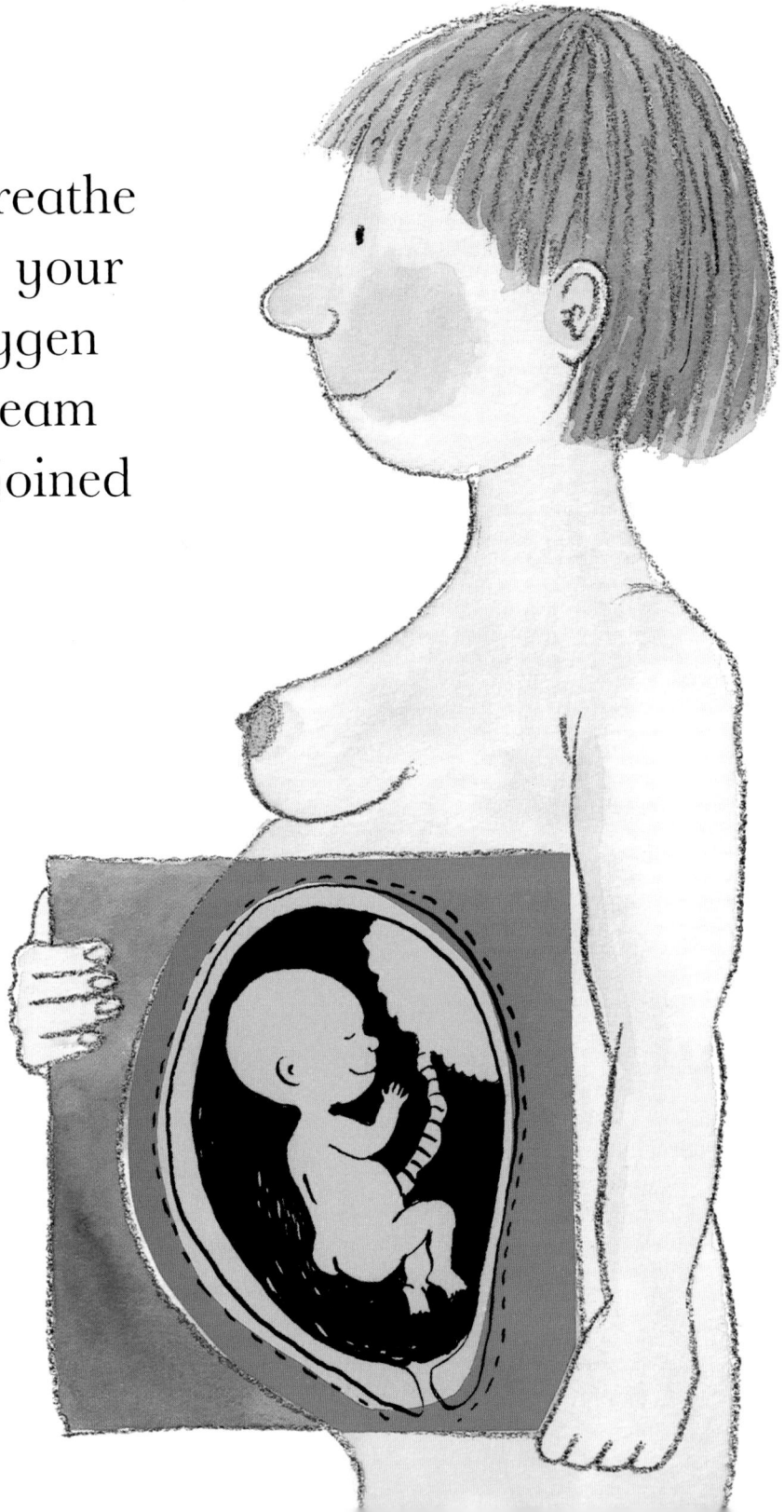

The tube is called an umbilical cord – that's where your belly button is now.

Mum's tummy stretched as you grew bigger. After five months she could feel you wriggling and kicking.

Sometimes you would play roly-poly in the middle of the night and wake your mum up!

You floated in a bag of warm water and all around was the echo of your mum's heart like a big drum!

Yes you could – when mum talked you could hear her. You could listen to music as well!

You could swim about. Sometimes you would drink some of the water you floated in – that would make you hiccup!

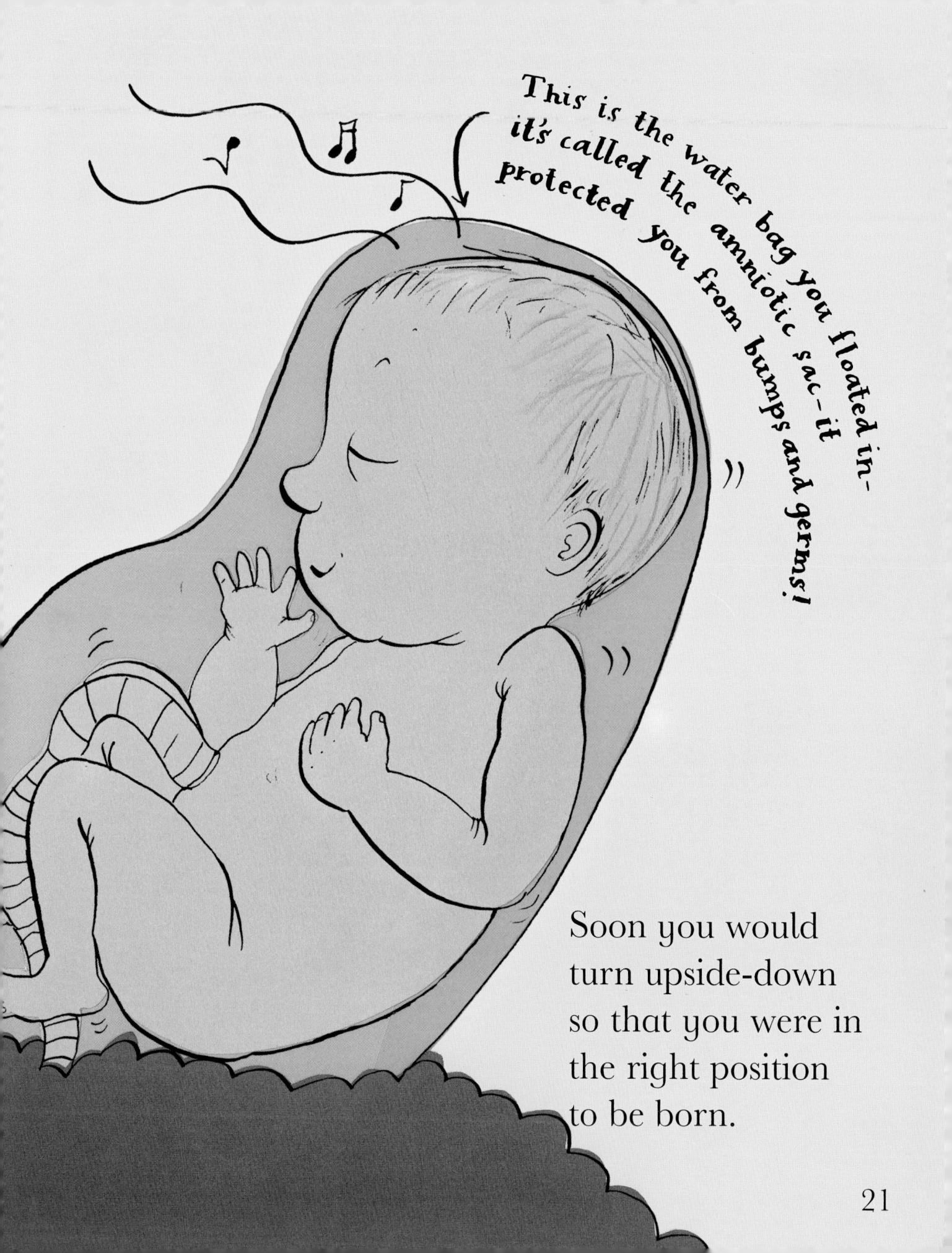

Soon you would
turn upside-down
so that you were in
the right position
to be born.

After about nine months your mum felt her tummy go tight, then relax. Gradually this feeling got stronger. This was the start of you being born – it's called labour.

Babies can be all sorts of sizes, but you were probably about the size of a rabbit!

The tight feelings your mum got in her tummy are called contractions. They can start hours before the birth will happen.

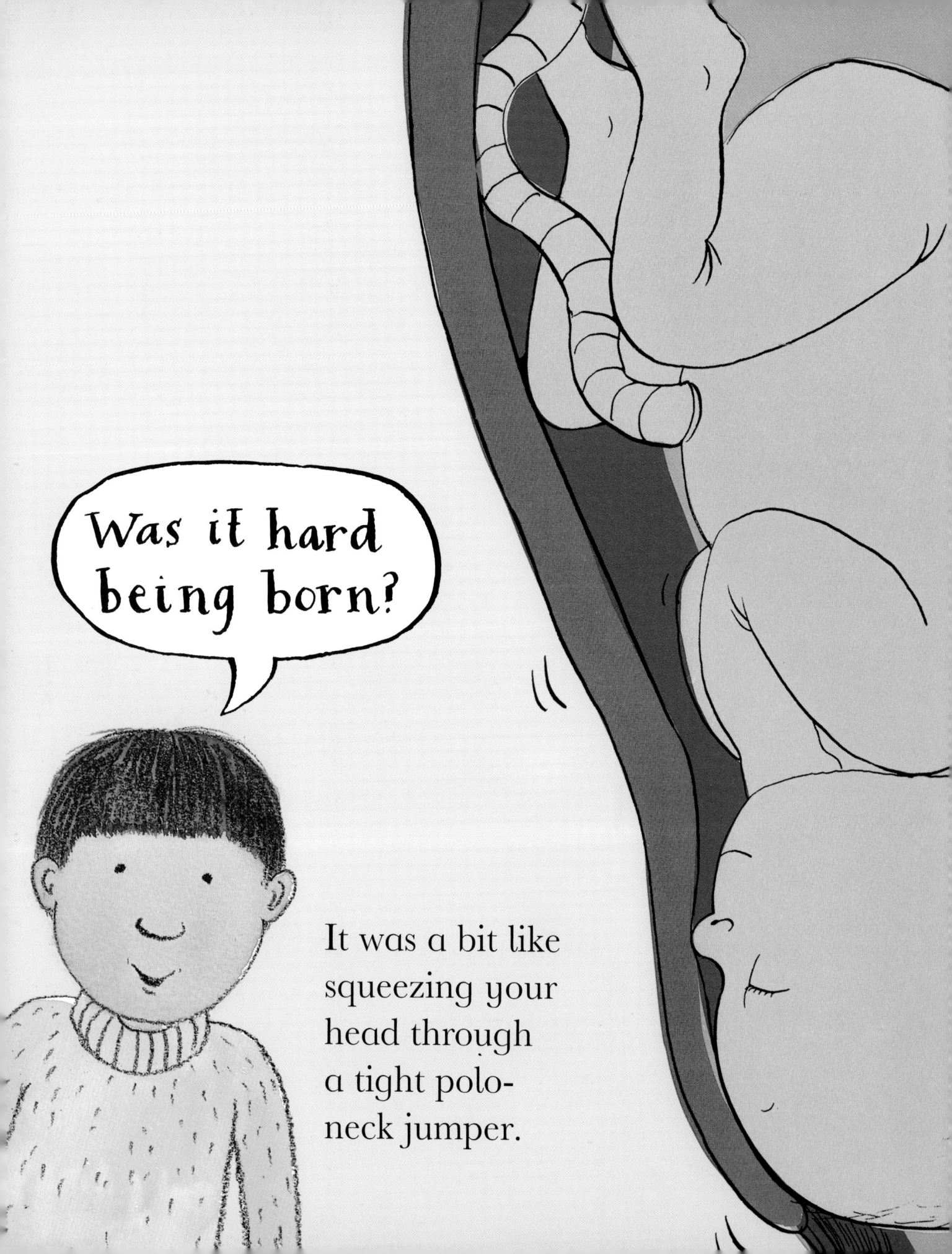

It was a bit like squeezing your head through a tight polo-neck jumper.

You were being squeezed out of your mum's womb. Suddenly the balloon of warm water you floated in burst! Slowly you were pushed out.

Sometimes babies can't be born like this, so a doctor puts mum to sleep and makes a small opening in her tummy and lifts the baby out – that is called a Caesarean.

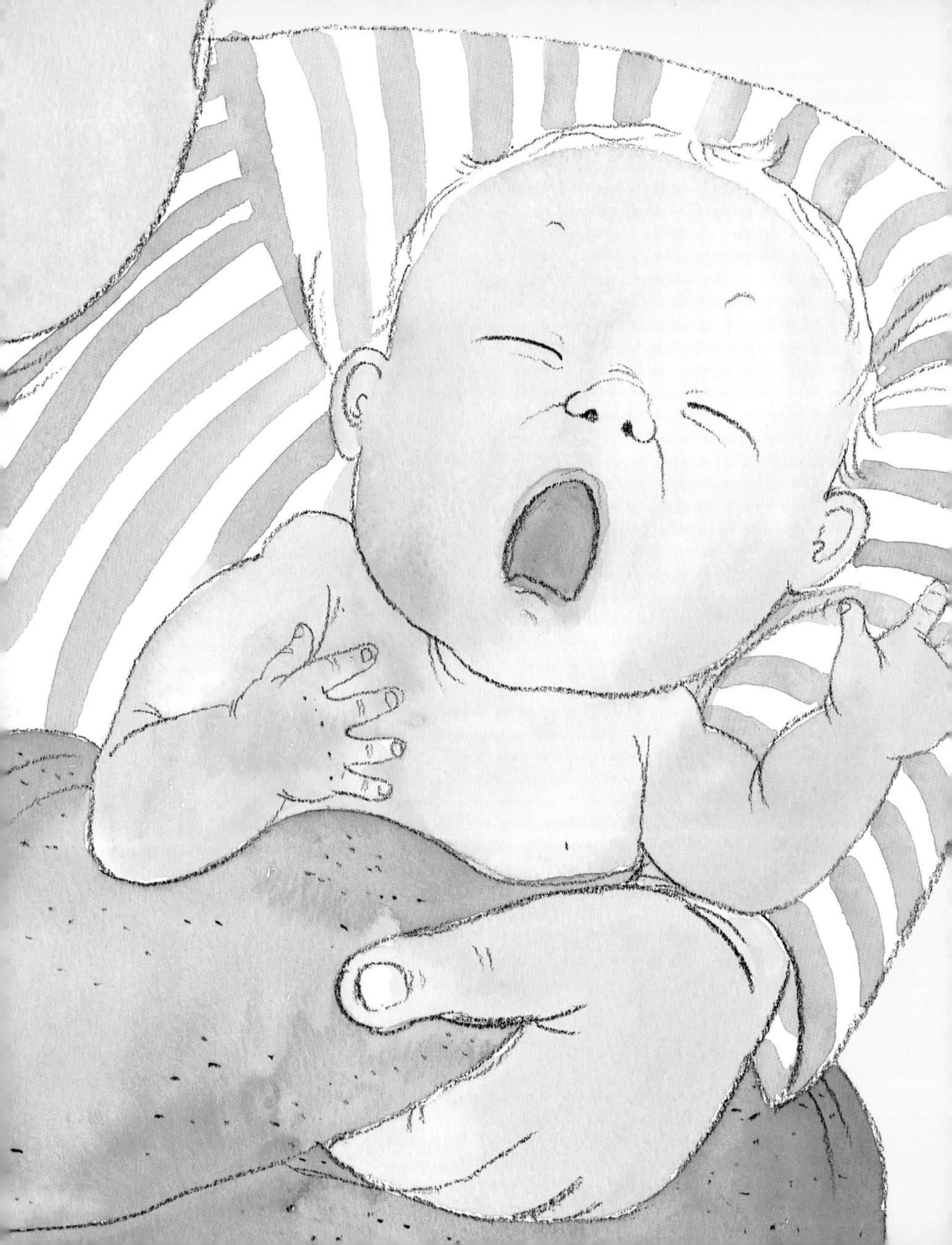

First everyone looked to see if you were a boy or a girl! Then someone cut the umbilical cord and weighed you.

You cried. Perhaps you wanted to be back in that warm place, listening to your mum's heartbeat or perhaps you just wanted to say hello!

How did I begin?

So you see you started with a cuddle between your mum and dad. Then nine months later there was you, a newborn baby sleepy in your mum's arms.

Now here you are looking at this book!

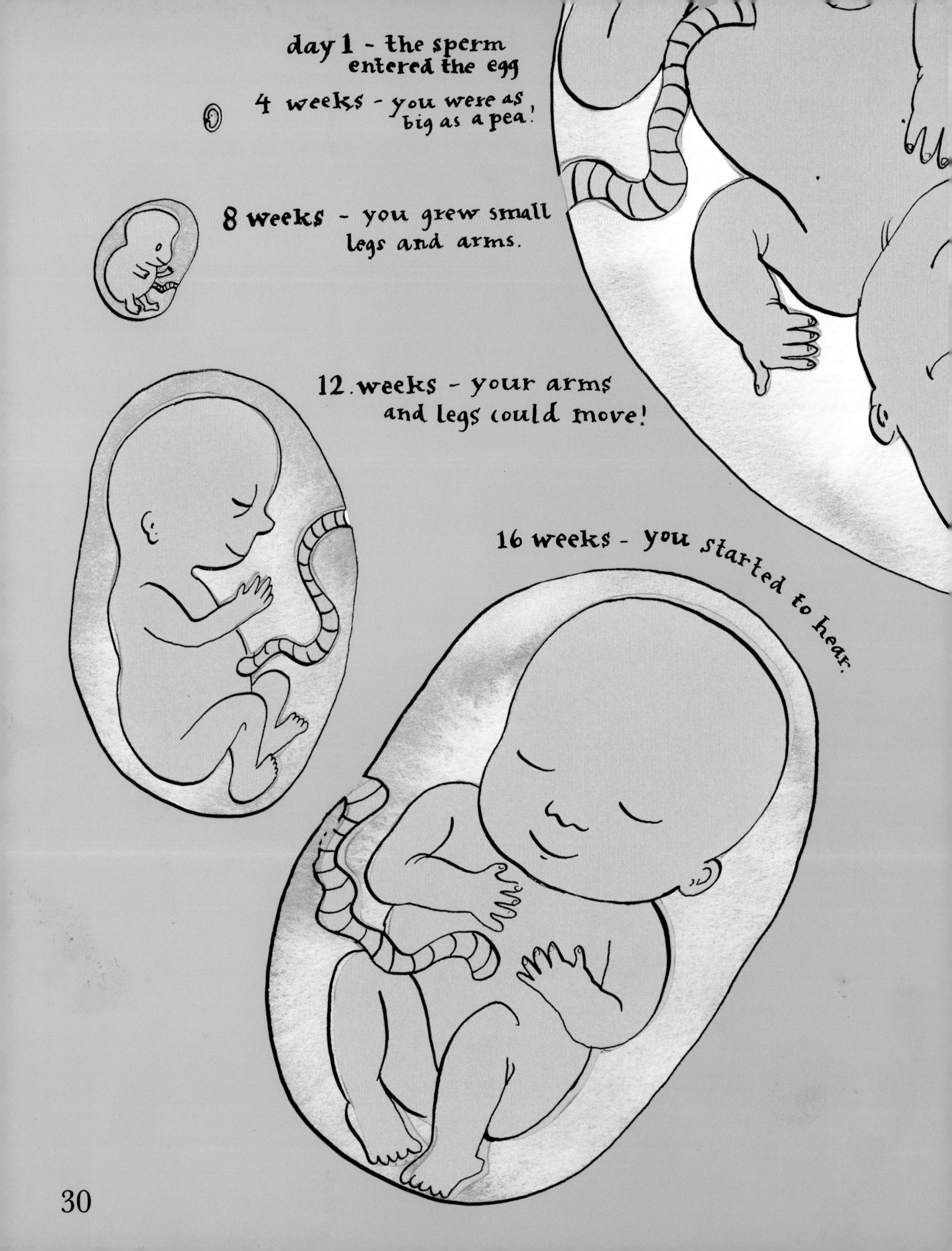
day 1 - the sperm entered the egg
4 weeks - you were as big as a pea!
8 weeks - you grew small legs and arms.
12 weeks - your arms and legs could move!
16 weeks - you started to hear.

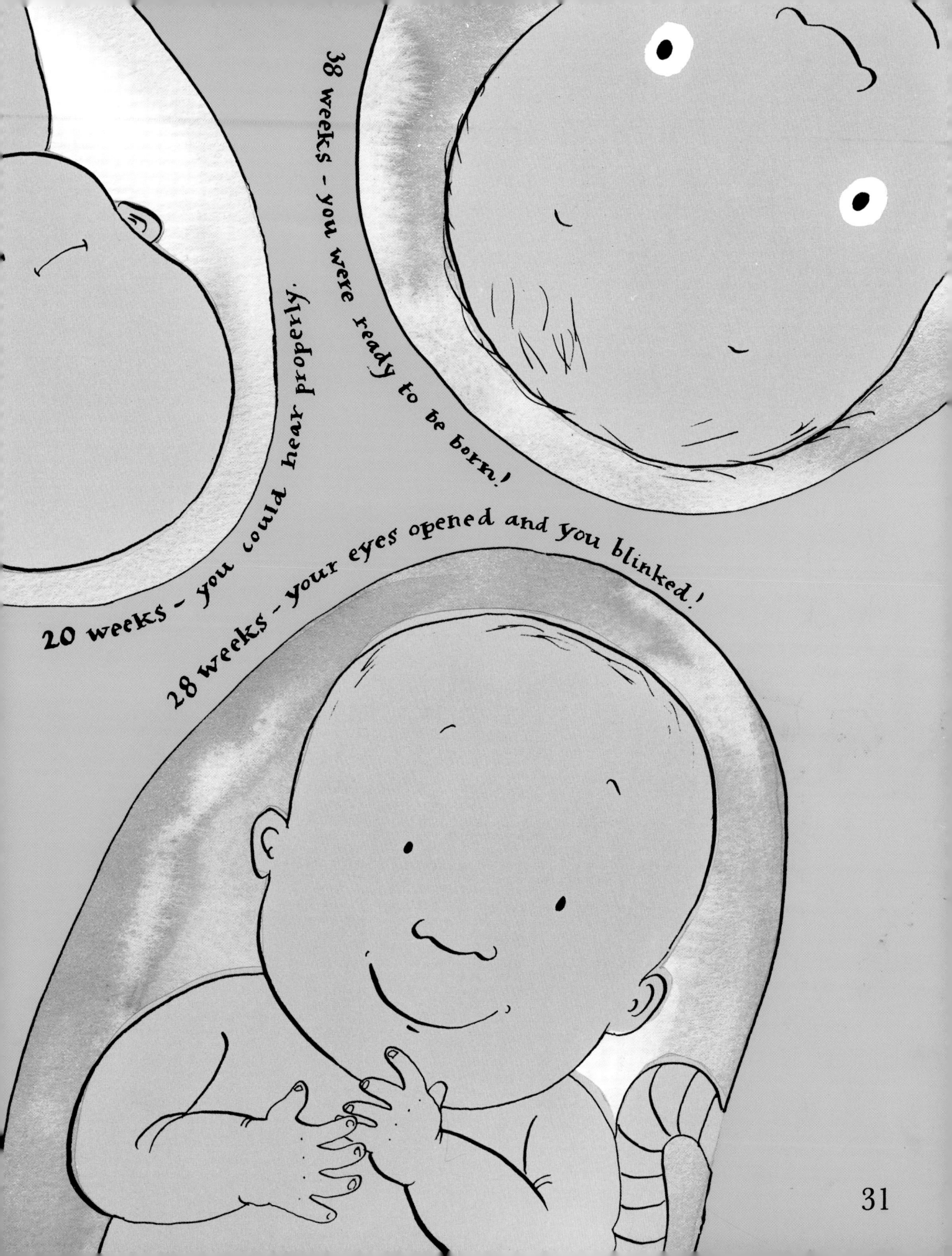
20 weeks - you could hear properly.
28 weeks - your eyes opened and you blinked!
38 weeks - you were ready to be born!

This edition 2004

First published in 1997, by Franklin Watts,
338 Euston Road
London NW1 3BH.

Franklin Watts Australia
Level 17/207 Kent Street
Sydney, NSW 2000

Text and illustrations © Mick Manning and Brita Granström 1997.
Editor: Paula Borton
Consultant: Belinda Ashon MB. BS MFFP
Printed in China
A CIP catalogue record is available
from the British Library.
Dewey Classification 612.6
ISBN 978 0 7496 5661 4

Franklin Watts is a division of
Hachette Children's Books.

For Charlotte